W9-BOL-673

Creative Podcast Producers

Heather C. Hudak

ABDOPUBLISHING.COM

Published by Abdo Publishing, a division of ABDO, PO Box 398166, Minneapolis, Minnesota 55439. Copyright © 2019 by Abdo Consulting Group, Inc. International copyrights reserved in all countries. No part of this book may be reproduced in any form without written permission from the publisher. Checkerboard Library™ is a trademark and logo of Abdo Publishing.

Printed in the United States of America, North Mankato, Minnesota
052018
092018

 THIS BOOK CONTAINS RECYCLED MATERIALS

Design: Kelly Doudna, Mighty Media, Inc.
Production: Mighty Media, Inc.
Editor: Liz Salzmann
Cover Photographs: iStockphoto (right), Shutterstock (left)
Interior Photographs: AP Images, pp. 15, 28 (top); Getty Images, p. 19; iStockphoto, pp. 7, 11, 13, 21, 23, 25, 26, 29 (top); Joi Ito/Flickr, pp. 17, 28 (bottom); Shutterstock, pp. 4, 9

Library of Congress Control Number: 2017961587

Publisher's Cataloging-in-Publication Data
Name: Hudak, Heather C., author.
Title: Creative podcast producers / by Heather C. Hudak.
Description: Minneapolis, Minnesota : Abdo Publishing, 2019. | Series: It's a digital world! | Includes online resources and index.
Identifiers: ISBN 9781532115318 (lib.bdg.) | ISBN 9781532156038 (ebook)
Subjects: LCSH: Podcasting--Juvenile literature. | Podcasts--Juvenile literature. | Occupations--Careers--Jobs--Juvenile literature.
Classification: DDC 006.7876--dc23

CONTENTS

Podcasts for Everyone 5

Podcast Preparation 6

Doing Many Jobs 8

Tools of the Trade. 10

At the Office 12

Podcast Past 14

Gaining Popularity 18

Making Money. 20

Podcasting Trends 24

Timeline 28

Glossary. 30

Online Resources 31

Index 32

PODCASTS FOR EVERYONE

Have you ever been on a road trip or a long flight?
Riding in a car or plane for hours can be really boring. Listening to podcasts is a great way to pass the time. Podcasts are digital audio files you can **download** or stream live. You can listen to them on a digital **media** player or smartphone. Most podcasts are similar to radio shows. They feature people talking about different subjects or telling stories.

Podcast producers are the people who make podcasts. They record audio, edit it, and then post it on the internet. There are podcasts on just about any topic you can think of. Some, such as *Tumble*, talk about cool science discoveries. Others, such as *Dream Big*, share celebrity interviews and urge kids to follow their dreams. Most podcasts have multiple episodes. Podcast producers work hard to make each episode interesting and entertaining.

CHAPTER 1

PODCAST PREPARATION

Podcast producers record and edit podcasts to be posted on the internet. Podcast producers have a strong interest in the themes of their podcasts. They may even be experts on the topics. Podcasts are a way to share their passion and excitement with others.

Podcast listeners can find information about topics that interest them. For example, there aren't many radio shows just about math. But people who love math can listen to the podcast *Math Mutation*. Its episodes are full of fun and weird math facts.

Most podcast producers have many different skills. Producers need to be well organized. They do a lot of different tasks and need to manage their time well. They need to have strong communication skills and pay attention to detail. They should also be good at solving problems and meeting due dates.

Podcast producers do not need to have college degrees. In fact, they do not need any special training at all. Anyone

Apple allows podcast producers to track when listeners start, stop, or skip during a podcast episode. This allows producers to better understand the types of content their listeners enjoy.

of any age and experience can create a podcast. All they need is a computer with a microphone and the internet.

However, some podcast producers are professionals. They have experience working in radio or other **media**. In those jobs, they use a lot of the same **software** and equipment podcasters use. They also learn interviewing and storytelling skills. Some podcast producers take courses to build their skills. Producers must keep up with new **technologies** as they come out.

CHAPTER 2

DOING MANY JOBS

A lot of work goes into making a podcast. Podcast producers perform research to learn about new ideas. They also look for exciting content and find interesting guests for their episodes.

Sometimes, podcast producers are also the hosts of their podcasts. They tell stories and interview guests. Other podcast producers are hired by podcast hosts to produce the podcasts.

It is the podcast producer's job to run the tools and equipment used to record and edit podcasts. They need to know how to use sound editing **software** to make the podcast sound good. This includes adding music and sound effects. It also includes removing stammers, mistakes, and any other unwanted content.

Podcast producers **upload** completed podcasts to websites or podcast hosting servers. Then, the producers must **market** their podcasts. They want to build **audiences** for their podcasts.

A successful podcast has many loyal listeners who listen to every episode.

Blogs and **social media** posts are common ways producers get the word out about their podcasts. In most cases, new episodes of a podcast come out at the same time each week or month. A podcast calendar is sometimes posted on a website so listeners can find out about upcoming topics and dates.

One of the best podcast promotion tools is ratings. Podcast apps allow users to rate podcasts. Higher ratings mean more listeners!

CHAPTER 3

TOOLS OF THE TRADE

Anyone can start a podcast if they have the right tools and equipment. Even kids can do it! Many schools encourage students to prepare podcasts for school projects.

Most new computers come with the basic **software** and equipment needed to produce a podcast. Computers have built-in microphones, or *mics*. A number of audio editing programs, such as GarageBand and Audacity can be **downloaded** for free. Using programs such as these is the most affordable way to get started.

There are tools people can buy to improve the quality of their podcasts. One of the most important pieces of equipment is the microphone. Each mic produces a different sound quality. Hosts need to find one that works well for them.

Another important tool for podcast producers is the audio software. Software programs are designed to record, create, edit, and mix podcasts. They are called digital audio workstations (DAWs). Examples of DAWs include Pro Tools and Adobe Audition.

GarageBand can also be used on iPads. Producers can even use this app to create their own music for the podcast.

After a podcast is recorded, the producer saves it as digital audio file, such as an MP3 file. Then the producer edits it. He or she can cut out mistakes, add special effects, and more.

When finished, the podcast is posted **online**. Some podcasts have websites listeners can **download** episodes from. Podcasts are also posted in online stores, such as iTunes and Google Play Music. Stitcher, Spotify, and other apps also provide podcasts.

CHAPTER 4

AT THE OFFICE

Podcast producers can work in different types of locations and situations. Often, producers can work anywhere in the world they want. They just need to have a strong internet connection and the proper **software** and equipment.

Many podcast producers work from their own homes. Some are **entrepreneurs** who write, edit, host, and **market** their own podcasts. They decide what they want to talk about and prepare their own content. No one tells them what to do or when to do it.

Other podcast producers work for a company or organization. These producers create podcasts related to the companies' products or services. Tour companies may use podcasts to

DIGITAL BIT

Podcast listeners listen to an average of five different shows per week. The most popular type of podcast is comedy. Education and news are the next most popular types.

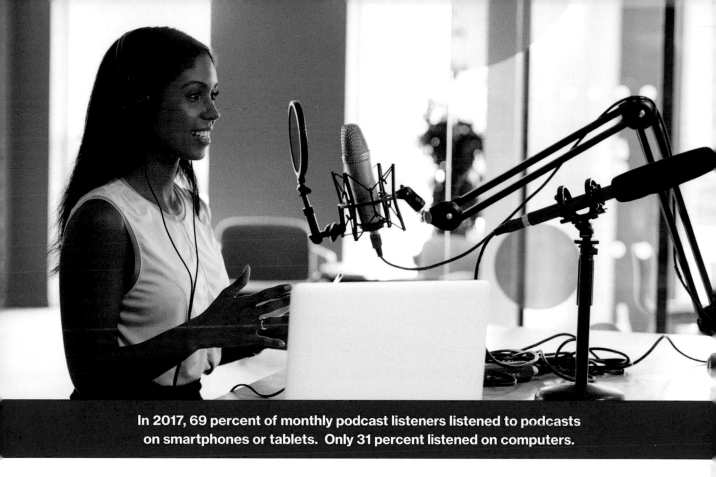

In 2017, 69 percent of monthly podcast listeners listened to podcasts on smartphones or tablets. Only 31 percent listened on computers.

talk about ideas for sightseeing. Educational companies may use podcasts to teach lessons.

Freelancing is another way for podcast producers to work. Instead of working full-time for one company, freelancers work on a project-by-project basis. Freelancers work with the people who hire them to produce the podcast.

CHAPTER 5

PODCAST PAST

No matter where podcast producers work today, the job has only existed for about 15 years. The World Wide Web (the web) was invented in 1989. Within a few years, radio producers started streaming their programs live on the web.

In 1995, the MP3 file format was released. This was a way to compress digital audio so it takes up less computer memory. It made storing more digital audio files possible. To create a digital, or MP3, file, the computer turns recorded sound into streams of numbers. When the MP3 is played, the computer turns the numbers back into sounds. **Bloggers** and radio broadcasters started adding MP3 files to their websites. Listeners could **download** the MP3 files and listen to them on their computers.

The first digital audio players came out in 1998. MP3 files could be transferred from computers onto digital audio players. This made it possible for people to listen to MP3 files without being tied to their computers. These early MP3 players were

Popular MP3 players in 2002 included (*left to right*) SONICblue's Rio Riot, Apple's iPod, and Creative Labs' Nomad Jukebox 3.

expensive and couldn't hold much content. Over time, the **technology** improved. MP3 players became less expensive. They also had more memory.

Soon, many people were buying MP3 players. One of the most popular brands was the Apple iPod. MP3 players were mostly used to listen to music. But people started thinking of ways to use MP3 files to share other types of content.

The development of RSS feeds paved the way for new types of audio sharing. RSS is a file format released in 1999. RSS uses keywords, or tags, to collect content on a specific topic from websites. Then it puts the content together in a list, called a feed. People interested in the topic can **subscribe** to the feed. New items are added to the feed when the websites post new content.

In 2000, **software** developer Dave Winer added a new element to RSS. It was the ability to include links to MP3 audio files in RSS feeds. This used a new type of RSS tag called an enclosure. Enclosures allowed RSS feeds to link to audio and video files.

In 2003, journalist and TV host Christopher Lydon produced an audio **blog** that included recordings of interviews with prominent scientists and politicians. Winer used RSS to create a feed of Lydon's interviews that listeners could subscribe to. The feed was updated as new interviews were added. Though the word podcast was not in use yet, Lydon's audio blog was just that. It was the first podcast.

DIGITAL BIT

The term "podcast" is a combination of the words "iPod" and "broadcast." Journalist Ben Hammersley first used the term in a 2004 issue of the *Guardian* newspaper.

Dave Winer has been called the father of blogging and RSS.

CHAPTER 6

GAINING POPULARITY

Podcasts started becoming popular thanks to Adam Curry. In 2004, Curry started producing a podcast called *The Daily Source Code*. In the podcast, he played music and talked about his life as well as current events.

The Daily Source Code was the first podcast that was more than a feed of audio files. Curry was the first to plan and produce a podcast that was similar to a radio show. Curry became known as the "Podfather."

Also in 2004, Liberated Syndication (Libsyn) became the first podcast service provider. Both new and experienced podcasters started using Libsyn to host and publish their podcasts. Today, more than 35,000 podcasts are hosted by Libsyn. Each month, about 62 million people listen to podcasts by Libsyn hosts.

In June 2005, Apple released a new **version** of its **online** music store, iTunes. For the first time, iTunes included podcasts.

This made it even easier for people to find their favorite podcasts. They could now **subscribe** and listen to podcasts on iTunes.

At first, there were 3,000 free podcasts on iTunes. New episodes were delivered to each subscriber's iPod or computer as they came out. At the time, iTunes was the main source of **downloadable** music. So, being included on iTunes provided a big **breakthrough** that helped many podcasters find success.

Before starting his podcast, Adam Curry was a TV personality on the music channel MTV.

CHAPTER 7

MAKING MONEY

For many podcast producers, success meant making money. One way for podcast producers to make money is by charging their **subscribers** a fee. However, this method requires a very large **audience** to be profitable.

Podcast producers can also make money by working with companies that have **online** stores. Podcast producers can sign up for **affiliate** programs with these companies. For example, many podcasters participate in online sales giant Amazon's affiliate program.

Amazon gives each podcaster a special code or website link to pass on to their listeners. Then, during podcasts, the hosts recommend products Amazon sells and passes

DIGITAL BIT

A podcast sponsor can pay to be mentioned at the beginning, middle, or end of the podcast. These are called pre-roll, mid-roll, or post-roll mentions. Mid-roll mentions are usually longer and more expensive than pre-roll or post-roll mentions.

Many podcasts have accounts on Patreon. This is a website where podcast listeners or other fans can support people's businesses.

on the codes. When someone orders from the store using a podcast's code, the podcast receives a portion of the sale amount.

Another way for podcast producers to make money is to sell their own products or services. Some podcasters write books or offer courses on different topics. Others make artwork or other items. Some podcasters sell T-shirts and other items featuring the name of their podcasts. Whatever the product, mentioning it during a podcast is a common way to advertise it.

However, the most common way podcasts make money is through **sponsors**. A sponsor is a company that pays to be mentioned on podcasts. Some companies want to sponsor podcasts that have the largest **audiences**. This way they will reach more customers.

However, many companies look to sponsor podcasts that are related to the company's products or services. What matters most to them is whether the audience will buy a product or service that is recommended on the podcast. A company may sponsor a podcast with loyal listeners, even if there are fewer of them. Loyal listeners are more likely to follow the advice of the podcast, such as buying certain products.

National Public Radio (NPR) is the top podcast producer. It offers dozens of podcasts. Some of its podcasts are episodes of radio shows. Others were developed as podcasts. Overall, NPR podcasts are **downloaded** more than 100 million times each month.

One of NPR's most popular podcasts is *Wow in the World*. It is a weekly podcast for kids that explores science and **technology**. It features fun topics, such as why onions make people cry and why squirrels hide nuts. The hosts include funny stories to draw in listeners and keep them coming back for more. The podcast started in May 2017. Since then, its episodes have been downloaded more than five million times!

CHAPTER 8

PODCASTING TRENDS

Podcasts are becoming more and more popular.
Between 2008 and 2017, the number of monthly podcast listeners in the US increased from 9 percent to 24 percent. In the past, people had to tune into radio and TV shows when they were broadcast. Today, the internet and **mobile** devices allow people to choose when to watch and listen to podcasts and other content. They can **download** podcasts and listen to them when they have free time.

Technology and trends are always changing, so podcast producers need to change right along with them. As new technologies are invented, producers can use them to make new and better podcasts. They need to continue learning about new **software** and experimenting with ways to use it.

Storytelling is one of the biggest podcasting trends. Podcasts are starting to use **narrative** to engage listeners. Instead of just talking about a topic, they are making it into a story.

Podcasts are especially popular because people can multitask with them. People can clean, work, or do other activities while listening to podcasts.

Experts think fictional podcasts will become more popular in the future. These include podcasts based on comic books, TV shows, and movies.

In some cases, the stories are make-believe. One fiction podcast is the children's podcast *The Alien Adventures of Finn Caspian*. Its first episode was produced in 2016. In other **narrative** podcasts, the stories are based on true events.

For example, *The Past & The Curious* explores history through storytelling and music.

Some podcast producers tell a full story in one episode. Others tell only part of the story in each episode. They end each episode with a **cliff-hanger**. Listeners have to tune in to the next episode if they want to find out how the story ends.

Another hot trend in podcasting is live video streaming. A live video stream is a video posted on the internet as it is being recorded. Some podcast producers use live video streaming to interact with their listeners. This allows listeners to watch podcasts being recorded. People watching the live video can ask podcast producers questions or give them **feedback** about their shows.

Many podcast producers are finding new ways to use their podcasting skills beyond podcasts, such as **narrating** audio books. As podcasts continue to grow, so will new opportunities for podcast producers to use their skills. Only time will tell what other creative ideas podcast producers will come up with!

TIMELINE

1989
The World Wide
Web is invented.

1998
The first digital audio
players come out.

1995
The MP3
file format
is released.

1999
The RSS file
format is
released.

2000
Dave Winer invents
RSS enclosures.

2003
Winer and Christopher Lydon create the first podcast.

2016
The first episode of
The Alien Adventures of
***Finn Caspian* is produced.**

2004
Adam Curry starts the podcast *The Daily Source Code*. Libsyn becomes the first podcast service provider.

2005
The iTunes store starts offering podcasts.

2017
The first episode of NPR's *Wow in the World* is released.

GLOSSARY

affiliate–a membership in or association with a company or organization.

audience–a group of readers, listeners, or spectators.

blog–a website that tells about someone's personal opinions, activities, and experiences. A person who writes a blog is a blogger.

breakthrough–a sudden advance or successful development.

cliff-hanger–a story, contest, or situation that is very exciting because what is going to happen next is not known.

download–to transfer data from a computer network to a single computer or device. Something that can be downloaded is downloadable.

entrepreneur–one who organizes, manages, and accepts the risks of a business or an enterprise.

feedback–information or criticism that suggests ways to improve something.

market–to advertise or promote something so people will want to buy it.

media–a form or system of communication, information, or entertainment. It includes television, radio, and newspapers.

mobile–capable of moving or being moved.

narrate–to tell a story. A story that is told in full detail is a narrative.

online–connected to the internet.

social media–forms of electronic communication that allow people to create online communities to share information, ideas, and messages. Facebook, Instagram, and Snapchat are examples of social media.

software–the written programs used to operate a computer.

sponsor– to pay for a program or an activity in return for promoting a product or a brand. Someone who does this is a sponsor.

subscribe–to agree to receive a publication and pay for it if it is not offered for free. Someone who does this is a subscriber.

technology (tehk-NAH-luh-jee)–machinery and equipment developed for practical purposes using scientific principles and engineering.

upload–to transfer data from a computer to a larger network.

version–a different form or type of an original.

INDEX

Adobe Audition, 10
affiliate programs, 20, 22
Alien Adventures of Finn Caspian, The, 26
Amazon, 20
Apple, 15, 18
Apple iPod, 15, 18
Audacity, 10

blogs, 9, 14, 16

computers, 7, 10, 14, 19
Curry, Adam, 18

Daily Source Code, The, 18
digital audio files, 11, 14, 15, 16
digital audio workstations, 10
digital media players, 5, 14, 15
Dream Big, 5

editing, 5, 6, 8, 10, 11, 12
education, 6, 10, 13

enclosures, 16
episodes, 5, 6, 8, 9, 11, 19, 23, 26, 27
equipment, 7, 8, 10, 12

GarageBand, 10
Google Play Music, 11

hosting, 8, 10, 12, 20, 23

internet, 5, 6, 7, 11, 12, 24, 27
interviews, 5, 7, 8, 16
iTunes, 11, 18, 19

Liberated Syndication, 18
live video streaming, 27
Lydon, Christopher, 16

marketing, 8, 9, 12
Math Mutation, 6
microphones, 7, 10
MP3 files, 11, 14, 15, 16
music, 8, 15, 18, 19, 27

National Public Radio, 23

Past & The Curious, The, 26, 27
Pro Tools, 10

radio, 5, 6, 7, 14, 23, 24
recording, 5, 6, 8, 10, 11, 14, 16, 27
research, 8
RSS feeds, 16

science, 5, 23
selling products, 22
software, 7, 8, 10, 12, 24
sponsorships, 22
Spotify, 11
Stitcher, 11
storytelling, 5, 7, 8, 24, 26, 27
subscribing, 16, 19, 20

Tumble, 5

websites, 8, 9, 11, 14, 16, 20
Winer, Dave, 16
World Wide Web, 14
Wow in the World, 23